You are Loved

A Prayer in Poetry, for the Child Within You

By

Dana Bradshaw

Just about everyone is recovering from traumatic events from childhood.

Unfortunately, pain follows us into adulthood. And, we are all recovering. This prayer, written in poetry is dedicated to the healing child inside. It was written to reach, heal and pry for the child within you.

A Dedication

I dedicate this book to *Kay Packard.*

She inspired me to pray and talk to the hurt child within me. I am

forever grateful for her. My gift to her is this book, in prayer for

the child within all of us.

Thank you, Kay.

You are loved

I pray to you almighty God,

with the power of the Holy Spirit,

that you feel God's absolute,

               Love.

A

               Love

So great that it will never die,

Fade

or be forgotten.

               Love

that reaches down

to the core of your existence.

A

               Love

that roots so deep

it grounds you.

So much, that you never feel

the need to seek

                    love

anywhere else.

So grounded,

that every step you take,

is secure in the fact your path

has already been,

signed,

sealed

and delivered by the heavenly father.

                    Love

So, lifting

that it carries the child inside of you

that has ever been,

abused,

abandoned,

hurt

or made to feel discarded.

                    Love,

so strong,

that every child knows that you are

Loved

and worthy of your magnificence.

For it is God's

Love

that will never forsake or leave.

I pray that you may feel an infinite light

 that reflects the illumination of God.

As he is,

Was

and always will be

this

Love

he has for you will be your infinite source

of strength

to overcome every obstacle,

challenge

or situation in your life.

Love

so great that,

you will never become weak,

as long as,

you are breathing.

 I pray that this

love

heals you of any pain,

trauma

and negativity

that exists due to childhood traumatic events,

situations

and unfortunate circumstances!

I pray all these things in the mighty name of Jesus!

Child, you are infinitely

and exponentially

Loved.

Amen.

You are Enough, More than Enough!

I pray to you almighty God,

with the power of the Holy Spirit,

that you let this child

feel so full of your greatness

that,

you will forever

feel so confident

you,

will always feel

more than enough,

self sufficient

by his grace.

Which is

more than enough.

That even

if you were

the last person

on earth,

he would send his only to save you!

 So worthy,

That your life

was chosen out of millions.

 It was

 and is

worth so much more

 that no value

 can be placed upon it.

Worth,

 so much,

 that Your life's purpose

was given

 to no

 one else but you.

It was worth,

 so much that death

was chosen

to save you.

You are infinitely

worthy

of sufficient grace.

You are the child of a king.

Your birthright

is that of

royalty.

So great,

the sun has kissed your skin

with an immeasurable shield of protection,

it can never be penetrated.

You were

and are worth

forever existing,

even if

it is in the essences.

That anytime,

you are made

to feel less,

that you

remember,

 your life

 was paid for

by the value

 of a life.

That

                              you are enough,

And,

                              are more than enough.

Child,

                    you are enough,

                     more than enough.

Amen.

You are Greater than Circumstance

I pray to you almighty God,

 with the power of the Holy Spirit,

that you let this child feel

so loved that no matter what,

you know,

You are not your

                              circumstances.

No matter if you are a strung out on drugs,

 broke,

 homeless

or jobless,

That you are not that

                              circumstance.

                              Circumstance

is temporary but,

You, child

are permanent in his eyes.

 I'll let you know

that no matter where

you are in your current moment,

you are still

in the midst,

of an unstoppable move from God.

That,

if you turn it all over to him

for a solution,

it only takes

a mustard seed

of faith,

to accomplish.

And, know that it is already done.

No matter

what you are going through,

it is God's

final say.

Seek him,

he shall do the miracles,

 that he promised.

So,

no matter how low you feel,

it is him,

 that will raise you,

 back up into your purpose.

 For it was him,

that chose you out of millions

 to walk this destiny,

 and,

                              circumstance

 will never deny,

 kill

or destroy that.

You were created

 in the likeness,

 of our savior,

and one man

is like all men.

Child,

you are not

circumstance,

you are worthy of all great things.

You are loved

And,

you are a child of God,

No matter,

who your mother

or father

are in the flesh.

You were chosen

and,

no

circumstance

can ever change that.

As long as,

you

can breathe,

you have a purpose.

You are the child of a king.

Child,

You are great and,

that

                         circumstance

 you found yourself in,

is not greater

than what created all things.

God.

Amen.

You are never Alone

I pray to you almighty God

with the power of the Holy Spirit,

 that you let this child

feel so filled

with his

love

 and presence,

 that you never feel

                               alone.

And every step

 you take

 is already

been ordered by him.

He has

 Already

 been there

 befor you

 and is,

and always will be.

As a reminder,

inhale and fill

your lungs

with the breathe

he gave you

and

the air

he created for you

to live.

And remember,

he is

here with

You.

Everything,

created on this earth,

Has all been

conceived

by his creation.

And,

as long as

you know that,

you will never be

                                    alone.

That

 every journey

 you take,

 the ground

 was his creation

 and

he is with you

every step.

Every,

tree,

 plant,

 bird

and life form

 living is

 for your greater

good.

And,

he created them

already knowing

what you need.

You are never

                    Alone.

Call out his name

and

he will answer

showing,

 his presence

in your life.

Child, you are never

                    alone.

God

has created

 all of these

 living things

 so,

you

would never be

                                    alone!

Today is your Gift

I pray to you almighty Go,

with the power of the Holy Spirit,

that you let this child feel

so fulfilled,

 in that fact of knowing,

 that his life

 was so important,

he gave you,

 another day

 to live it.

That is his

                              Gift,

to you child.

The present of today.

 If you

 have never

 been given

 a

                    gift

before,

that the

                    gift

of today

 is

eternally

enough.

I pray

 That

You, child

 realize the

                    gift

of

now.

You

have been

                gifted

every second,

minute,

hour

and day,

to walk

in the purpose before

you.

You are so

needed,

 wanted

and loved

that you,

 have been awarded

today

 to live.

 And

live so fully

 that the

                              gift

of today

is never

•   wasted

or misused.

Child,

today is your

                              gift,

be grateful,

and know

that your life

has been blessed

with another chance

to live it.

Today is your

                              gift.

Amen.

Forever my Prayer for the child within you

I Pray that you know

You are infinitely Loved

That you know

You are Enough, More than Enough

And, that you

You are Greater than Circumstance

You are never Alone

Today is your Gift